Helping Children with Feelings

Helping Children who have Hardened their Hearts or Become Bullies

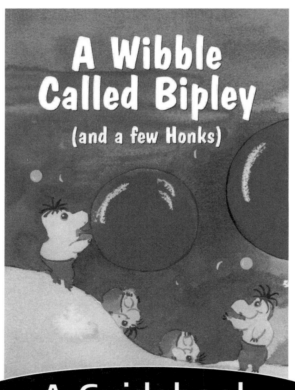

A Wibble Called Bipley (and a few Honks)

A Guidebook

Margot Sunderland

Illustrated by

Nicky Armstrong

Speechmark Publishing Ltd
Telford Road, Bicester, Oxon OX26 4LQ, UK

Note on the Text
For the sake of clarity alone, throughout the text the child has been referred to as 'he' and the parent as 'she'.

Unless otherwise stated, for clarity alone, where 'mummy', 'mother' or 'mother figure' is used, this refers to either parent or other primary caretaker.

Confidentiality
Where appropriate, full permission has been granted by adults, or children and their parents, to use clinical material. Other illustrations comprise synthesised and disguised examples to ensure anonymity.

Published by
Speechmark Publishing Ltd, Telford Road, Bicester, Oxon OX26 4LQ, UK
www.speechmark.net

First published 2000
Reprinted 2003, 2004

Text copyright © Margot Sunderland, 2000
Illustrations copyright © Nicky Armstrong, 2000

002-5061/Printed in the United Kingdom/1010

British Library Cataloguing in Publication Data
Sunderland, Margot
    A Wibble Called Bipley and a few Honks : helping children who have hardened their hearts or become bullies.
    Guidebook. – (Stories for Troubled Children)
    1. Storytelling – Therapeutic use 2. Child psychology 3. Learning, Psychology of
    I. Title II. Armstrong, Nicky
    615.8'516

ISBN 0 86388 458 X

(previously published by Winslow Press Ltd under ISBN 0 86399 299 4)

Contents

ABOUT THE AUTHOR

MARGOT SUNDERLAND is Founding Director of the Centre for Child Mental Health, London. She is also Head of the Children and Young People Section of The United Kingdom Association for Therapeutic Counselling. In addition, she formed the research project, 'Helping Where it Hurts' which offers free therapy and counselling to troubled children in several primary schools in North London. She is a registered Integrative Arts Psychotherapist and registered Child Therapeutic Counsellor, Supervisor and Trainer.

Margot is also Principal of The Institute for Arts in Therapy and Education – a fully accredited Higher Education College running a Diploma course in Child Therapy and Masters Degree courses in Arts Psychotherapy and Arts in Education and Therapy.

Margot is a published poet and author of two non-fiction books – one on *Dance* (Routledge Theatre Arts, New York and J Garnet Miller, England) and the other called *Draw on Your Emotions* (Speechmark Publishing, Bicester and Erickson, Italy).

ABOUT THE ILLUSTRATOR

NICKY ARMSTRONG holds an MA from The Slade School of Fine Art and a BA Hons in Theatre Design from the University of Central England. She is currently teacher of trompe l'œil at The Hampstead School of Decorative Arts, London. She has achieved major commissions nationally and internationally in mural work and fine art.

ACKNOWLEDGEMENTS

A special acknowledgement to Mattan Lederman who, at age seven, drew an entire set of pictures for all of the five stories in the pack. Several of his ideas and designs were then adopted by the illustrator.

I would like to thank Katherine Pierpont, Charlotte Emmett and Ruth Bonner for all their superb skill and rigour in the editing process, and for making the long writing journey such a pleasurable one.

I would also like to thank all the children, trainees and supervisees with whom I have worked, whose poetry, images and courage have greatly enriched both my work and my life.

ABOUT THIS GUIDEBOOK

If a child is going to benefit from the full therapeutic potential of *A Wibble Called Bipley (and a few Honks)*, this accompanying guidebook will be a vital resource. We strongly advise that you read it before reading the story itself to the child. By doing so, you will come to the child from a far more informed position, and so you will be able to offer him a far richer, and more empathic, response.

This guidebook details the common psychological origins and most relevant psychotherapeutic theories for the problems and issues addressed in the story. If you read it before reading the story to the child, it will prevent your coming to the child from an ignorant or closed viewpoint about why he is troubled. For example, 'I'm sure that Johnny's school work has gone downhill because he is missing his Daddy, who moved out a few months ago' may be an accurate or inaccurate hypothesis. There may be many other reasons for Johnny's problems in his school work, which have not been considered. The problem may well be complex, as so many psychological problems are. Coming from a closed or too narrow viewpoint all too often means that the helping adult is in danger of projecting on to the child *their own* feelings and views about the world.

Very few parents are consciously cruel. When something goes wrong in the parenting of a child, it is often to do with the parent *not knowing* about some vital aspect of child psychology or child development, or a lack in the way the parent was brought up themselves. There is still a tragic gap between what is known about effective parenting in child psychology, psychotherapy and scientific research, and how much of this is communicated to parents via parenting books or through television and the press. So this guidebook is not about blaming parents. Rather, the aim is to support. More generally, the aim is to heighten the awareness of *anyone* looking after children about how things can go wrong (usually despite the best intentions), and about how to help them go right in the first place, or to get mended if they do go wrong.

This guidebook includes what children themselves have said about what it is like trying to cope with the problems and issues addressed in the story, and describes the stories they have enacted through their play. It includes a section that offers suggestions and ideas for things to say and do after you have read *A Wibble Called Bipley (and a few Honks)* to the child. The suggestions and ideas are specifically designed to help a child to think about, express and further digest his feelings about the particular problems and issues addressed in the story. Some of the exercises are also designed to inspire children to speak more about what they are feeling through *their own* spontaneous story-making.

Everyday language is not the natural language for children to use to speak about what they feel. But, with an adult they trust, they can usually show or enact, draw or play out their feelings very well indeed. Therefore many of the exercises offered in this guidebook will support the child in creative, imaginative and playful ways of expressing himself. Also, so that you avoid asking too many questions, interrogating the child about his feeling life (to which children do not respond at all well), some of the exercises simply require the child to tick a box, 'show me', or pick a word or an image from a selection.

INTRODUCTION

> Our walls are our wounds – the places where we feel we can't love any more. (Williamson, 1992, p95)

What the story is about

Bipley is a warm, cuddly, little creature. The trouble is, someone has broken his heart. He feels so hurt that he decides that it is too painful to ever love again. Then when he meets some big tough Honks in the wood, they teach him how to harden his heart so that he does not have to feel hurt any more.

Bipley then turns into a bully. To begin with, he feels very powerful, but gradually he realises that his world has gone terribly grey. Luckily, however, Bipley meets some creatures who teach him how he can protect himself without hardening his heart. When he then makes the choice to dare to love again, although at first he is in pain, soon the warmth and colour come flooding back into his world. He is no longer alone.

The main psychological messages in the story

Walls around your heart can end up like a prison rather than just a mode of self-protection. Walls around your heart may keep out the harsh and the hurtful, but they can also stop good things such as warmth, love and kindness coming in. If you harden your heart, you may not experience much pain any more, but you may not experience much life either. Walls around your heart protect, but they also obstruct the view and keep out the light. Hardening your heart as a defence can be too effective in keeping people out.

> A person who does not feel, is one not sought out by others. (Polster, 1987, p305)

When you lose your capacity to love, the world can go terribly grey. You can find far less drastic ways of protecting yourself from too much emotional pain than by hardening your heart. If you close your heart to love, life can lose its meaning. Giving your life over to power is ultimately dissatisfying. Revenge is not sweet when it ruins your life.

> The pain of the past . . . cannot be erased by a fortress built today. (Blume, 1990, p49)
>
> When the walls are down, the world can expand. (Chopra, 1990, p230)

Who the story is for

This story was written for the following children:

★ Children who bully.

★ Children who have been too hurt in love.

★ Children who have become very defensive because something too painful has happened to them.

★ Children who have hardened their hearts because at home or at school they have met with too much harshness.

★ Children who have hardened their hearts because they have witnessed parental violence.

★ Children who have hardened their hearts because they have been repeatedly hit.

★ Children who have hardened their hearts because they have been shamed or humiliated.

★ Children who have hardened their hearts because of too many experiences of not being responded to.

★ Children who have hardened their hearts because they think they have lost their parent's love to someone else.

★ Children who take revenge on others for the pain they have felt themselves.

WHAT LIFE IS LIKE FOR A CHILD WHO HAS HARDENED HIS HEART

Building walls around your heart can mean self-imposed emotional poverty

> I'll stay down here! It'll be no use their putting their heads down and saying 'Come up again, dear!' . . . but, oh dear!' cried Alice, with a sudden burst of tears, 'I do wish they would put their heads down! I am so very tired of being all alone here! (Lewis Carroll, *Alice's Adventures in Wonderland*, 1865, pp15–16)

Children who have hardened their hearts usually suffer from a self-imposed emotional poverty. This is represented in the story when Bipley suddenly realises, after he has hardened his heart, that his world has gone completely grey. When a person becomes very defended in order to fend off emotional pain, he also keeps out all the emotionally nourishing things in life. Walls stop hurt coming in, but they also stop human warmth, love and kindness coming in. Also, giving good things out is one of the most emotionally nourishing things a person can do. However, if your whole being is set up as a system of defence, geared to keeping out the hurtful and the bad, you are unlikely to want to give anything lovely to anybody. You are in a completely different mind set.

If a child has a defence of being hard and tough like Bipley, it means that he also often shuts out the possibility of help. The messages he gives out of 'I don't need you', or 'I don't need' are often so strong that people just accept them at face value. Thus the walls around his heart can end up more like a prison than a mode of self-protection. Some people may persevere with such children for a while, in the hope that the walls will melt, but the majority will eventually leave for a 'warmer climate' – metaphorically speaking.

If you close your heart and choose power over love, life becomes harsh and bleak

> Simon, aged ten, had hardened his heart when his Daddy left him. In Simon's story, the lonely polar bear said 'I keep myself in a cold place, but at least I feel safe.'

Figure 1
Before he was a Honk, Bipley also knew these lovely relationship experiences

In the Wibble story, when Bipley became a tough Honk, his relationships became control-based and power-based rather than affection-based. If that happens to a child, it can be very bleak. A power-based world – that is a world where one's primary mode of relating is either, 'You have power over me', or 'I have power over you' – is a world where, metaphorically speaking, there is no sun and there are no leaves on the trees. It is as if it is always winter.

A child who lives in a power-based world can miss out on much that is emotionally enriching and life-enhancing. He misses out on the softer, gentler and lighter ways of being with other people, such as interactions of gentleness, calmness, warmth and cosiness. For example, the lovely relationship experiences that AA Milne describes so well in *Winnie-the-Pooh* are not available to him.

> When you've been walking in the wind for miles, and you suddenly go into somebody's house, and he says, 'Hallo, Pooh, you're just in time for a little smackerel of something', and you are, then it's what I call a Friendly Day. (Milne, 1926)

In their play, sooner or later, these children who have chosen power over love will show you a harsh inner world. You are likely to see endless bombings, killings, suffocations, drownings, bloody wars, sometimes all ending up in some futile heap of annihilated figures. Then there are also often the very weak, defenceless creatures getting shot, blown up, strangled, decapitated, or horribly menaced. The absence of any figures of tenderness, concern, kindness, help or support is very marked in the stories of these children (see Figure 2).

Figure 2
A drawing of a sandplay story of a child's harsh inner world. This was done by Peter, aged 6. It is a story about a living hell on earth, where no-one is safe, and there is always a threat. Note the absence of anything warm, kind or safe.

How people tend to avoid or to respond in harsh ways to children who have hardened their hearts

> As we build walls around our own heart, we indeed create our own hell. (Jeffers, 1987, p78)

Children who have hardened their hearts are often very difficult to be with. They usually present as either under-aroused or over-aroused energetically. That is, their defence system has rendered them either flat and dulled or hyperactive, aggressive, harsh, loud or over-the-top. Many children who have hardened their hearts are also seen as unkind. This is very understandable. As such children are defending themselves against their own vulnerable feelings, they are highly unlikely to be able to empathise with those of others. Their defences block them not only from their own feelings, but from those of others. This again makes relationships difficult with anyone other than someone hard and tough like themselves. This is what happened to Bipley who, when he hardened his heart, lost all his Wibble friends and was left with only the Honks.

Aggressively-defended adults and children who show no vulnerability; who therefore have a limited range of emotional energy states, and a very limited range of relational options, are usually wearing to be with. Their manner says 'See how big and tough and invulnerable I am!', but the absence of anything gentle, tender, warm and open can make people want to move away very quickly or not want to connect in the first place. Tough, hard children continually bring out something hard and tough in the people they meet. Many people feel so provoked, that they move into a very punishing reaction. And because children who have hardened their hearts rarely evoke a kind or warm response in another person, this makes the situation all the worse for them. Because of the cold responses they get, these very defended children feel even more justified in shutting themselves off in such a harsh, unkind world. Consequently their emotional pain underneath gets more and more hidden from their social world.

The problem is that people just see the behaviour, the defence of the child, the toughie. They do not see his pain underneath. In most interactions, they meet the child's wall, rather than the child behind the wall. Consequently, any real connection cannot happen. When people say about such children, 'I can't reach him,' they mean they cannot connect with the child, they only come up against his defences. Or, when a teacher or parent says, 'I don't actually like my child/that child,' it is the child's defences that they do not like, not the child himself. They may never have actually 'met' or got to know the child behind his defences. But it is common for both teachers and parents to confuse the child with his walls, and to think that is all there is. (The child himself may also begin to think that his defence is all he is, particularly if he has cut himself off from his tender, vulnerable, gentle feelings too successfully for too long.)

The child who shuts others out is not bad. He is desperately hurt and/or desperately frightened. 'That horrible child' is not horrible at core. His defences may be horrible and spiky, but that is because he thinks he needs to be like that in a world which he has experienced as too harsh, frightening or hurtful to be otherwise. But if anyone, such as a relative, teacher or counsellor, takes the time to wade through the monster tendrils, the spiky barbed wire of a child's defence system, they will usually find a vulnerable, frightened or terribly hurt little child underneath, just as is in the Bipley story. But you have to do the wading as soon as possible. With some teenagers, the cement of the defences around their heart has set so hard, and been there for so long, that it is extremely difficult to reach the hurt child underneath.

Without help, children who have hardened their hearts can become more and more unreachable, until most people stop trying to reach out to them at all – stop trying to make a connection. Why should they if, every time they do, they end up feeling rejected and shut out? The 'Keep Out' message is such a strong one. Very few people hang around for long.

Everyone can relate to the fact that there are children who move you and children who do not. The problem is that the latter often need far more attention than the former, but tend not to get it, because they present themselves in such unattractive or antisocial ways. The children who move you are the ones who have not closed their hearts. Big, tough, hard children only move people if their defences are not working well and so they are leaking their more vulnerable feelings (see *A Nifflenoo Called Nevermind*, Sunderland & Armstrong, 2000).

Mike, aged eleven

Mike's over-stretched mother was often very harsh with him. (Her own father had been very harsh with her.) Mike's mother's boyfriend had beaten up Mike on several occasions. Mike had often asked his mother to play with him, but she usually said she was too busy. One day, he stopped asking her any more.

Mike kept people out with his army-like camouflage clothes, his threatening talk, his large leather boots, the open safety-pins all over his clothes, and his favourite stance of legs apart, hands on hips. It was a convincing disguise that hid the frightened, very hurt little Mike underneath. He locked himself inside himself in a vain attempt to lock the hurt infant parts of himself deep within.

The security of a shut-in-life. (Bachelard, 1969, p115)

What life is like for children whose hurt has led them to prefer aloneness

> Myrtle complained that it was as difficult to find a way in to see me as to the Sleeping Beauty. I apologised but secretly I was pleased. Let it be difficult. Let it be like that for a hundred years. Prince Charming wasn't coming and no one else need bother. (Thrail, 1994, p159)

These are children who prefer to play on their own, rather than with other children, who for much of the time prefer to live in a private world of one, because a shared world has been so painful. As one ten-year-old girl who had hardened her heart said, 'I don't want a friend. We'd only argue.' These are children who, as Gianna Williams (1997) says, 'idealise places of desolation'. Two examples of such children are given below:

Sandy, aged eleven

Sandy's mother was loving one minute, then shouting and enraged the next. She often drank too much. When his teacher asked Sandy where he would most like to be if he could be anywhere, he said 'On the moon.' When asked why, he said, 'Because there are no people on it.'

Roger, aged twelve

Roger was a loner. His mother had died three years before. His father hit him a lot. In counselling Roger drew a bridge, then he drew himself walking across it. When he was safely across, he blew up the bridge. 'I blow up my bridge,' he said, 'So no one can cross it. In the past, people have crossed my bridge. So that is why I'm blowing it up.' In counselling, Roger was terrified of me 'getting inside his head'. It was safest, from Roger's hurt child perspective, to keep all people out. He simply did not feel strong enough to defend himself in any less drastic way, in case people abandoned him (his mother) or invaded him (his father).

But, for such children, their choice of aloneness can mean that their personal and emotional development can come to a complete standstill. Their defences mean that they live a small, tight version of life, where whole areas of their potential cannot be fulfilled.

An essential part of personal development is daring to be in a close relationship. Full participation in life, and tasting its riches, must include daring to let someone in, daring to let them matter, daring to let them become precious. 'I touch you, I talk to you, I smile at you, I see you, I ask you, I receive you, I know you, I want you – all in their turn support vibrancy in living. I am alone, yet to live I must meet you' (Polster & Polster, 1973, p99). But these are children who have been too hurt to risk this again.

Keeping walls around your heart can be very expensive in terms of time and energy

> George was now standing in a corner, as far away from his father as possible. A long time ago he had made up his mind to keep a really close watch on everything lest he should ever, by some devious means, either from behind or from above, be caught by surprise. (Kafka, 1981, p54)

The maintaining of major defences, needing to be on guard all the time to stop yourself feeling any more hurt, fear, grief, shame and so on, takes up large amounts of emotional energy. Any relaxation or distraction from the upkeep of the walls is experienced as far too risky: who knows who is trying to sneak up and invade, or attack or hurt you when you are off guard for a moment?

In short, children who have been 'too hurt' often live in a paranoid universe, where they are convinced it will happen again. No one can really be trusted. When you are hiding behind the battlements, you are not free to get on with anything else. In other words, psychic energy is given over to defence, rather than to getting on with living, and with enjoying life. Defences therefore use up vital life-force that could be spent far more creatively and in far more nourishing ways.

UNDERSTANDING WHY CHILDREN HARDEN THEIR HEARTS OR TURN TO BULLYING

Why children resort to hardening their hearts, and how the defence system works

For a child, the drastic defence of hardening his heart against feeling hurt again – against the pain of unrequited love or unmet need, unbearable loss or states of helplessness – is used as a desperate measure, an emergency defence system. This is because a child can feel attacked by the sheer level of the physiological arousal of his emotional pain. What eventually comes out (through therapy or counselling) in the stories of many children who have hardened their hearts is just how awful their level of emotional pain has been; how they have felt almost smashed up by it, blown up by it, shattered into bits by it. Many such children use images like this in their stories. In other words, the level of the child's emotional pain has felt like a threat to his survival, and so he is intensely frightened of feeling anything like that ever again. Hence too painful feelings must be cut off from. This means cutting off from spontaneous expansive, warm responses to the world, and just having tight little hard responses instead (see Figure 3).

Two common defences a child uses to harden his heart are desensitisation (a defence of emotional numbing) or repression (a defence of forgetting that you ever felt any pain in the first place). So for children like Bipley, their openness and vulnerability (which meant they got so hurt), have led them to try to be the opposite – invulnerable. With the effective defences of desensitisation or repression, the child can honestly say that he does not feel hurt or register emotional pain.

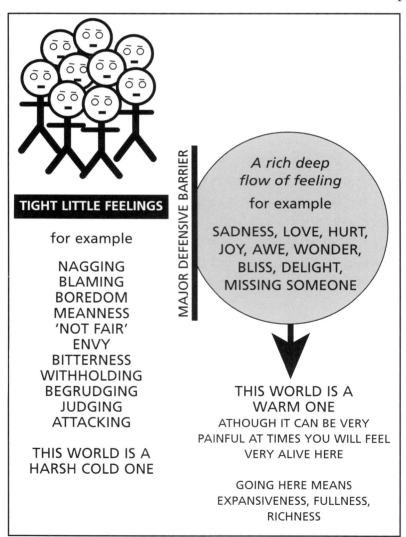

TIGHT LITTLE FEELINGS

for example

NAGGING
BLAMING
BOREDOM
MEANNESS
'NOT FAIR'
ENVY
BITTERNESS
WITHHOLDING
BEGRUDGING
JUDGING
ATTACKING

THIS WORLD IS A HARSH COLD ONE

MAJOR DEFENSIVE BARRIER

A rich deep flow of feeling for example

SADNESS, LOVE, HURT, JOY, AWE, WONDER, BLISS, DELIGHT, MISSING SOMEONE

THIS WORLD IS A WARM ONE
ATHOUGH IT CAN BE VERY PAINFUL AT TIMES YOU WILL FEEL VERY ALIVE HERE

GOING HERE MEANS EXPANSIVENESS, FULLNESS, RICHNESS

Figure 3 Tight little feelings

Children who harden their hearts because they could not get someone to love them

No, do thy worst, blind Cupid, I'll not love. (Shakespeare, *King Lear*, I, 20, v.132)

The obstacles to get to my mother were just too difficult. (Trudy, aged 14)

I so desperately wanted a loving mother, but all I got was a wall, so I think that after a while, I became a wall too. (Eileen, aged 16)

After too many desperate, but unsuccessful attempts to find something reliably loving in his parent – something warm in her tone, some gentle touch just for him – it is all too easy for a child to cut himself off and harden his heart. It is all to easy for him to say to himself, 'That love stuff is so sissy. I'm a big boy now. I don't need it any more.' It is all too easy for him to stop approaching his mother for hugs; to stop wanting to cuddle up to her in front of the television; to stop telling her he loves her; to stop bringing her little love gifts.

Sometimes it is a parent's inconsistency ('she loves me, she loves me not') that is the trigger. For other children, it is the mother's too few times of actual overt expressions of love. This is where love is felt, but not expressed. As one woman said, 'I had to go into therapy when I realised I couldn't tell my son that I loved him.' For a few children, their mother has never bonded with them, and so there have never been any expressions of love. The mother operates from a place of duty, and hopes one day that she will come to love her child. Some mothers are experienced by their child as loving, but then too often comes a terrible change in her, when he does something that triggers her into releasing bottled-up fury. She changes in an instant, and shouts at him in a frightening way or hits him: his loving mother has suddenly become a hitting one or a hating one. He is left with a terrible hurt, confusion and shock at the rupture between them. He feels deeply betrayed because he had trusted her with his love. So, over time, he hardens his heart and says 'Stuff it' to love.

Many people do not realise that broken hearts can actually be as common in babies and children as they are in adults. Infant–mother research shows that babies have the capacity to love their parents deeply, and so are just as vulnerable as adults to getting devastatingly hurt in that love (see Stern, 1993).

The (usually unconscious) decision made in childhood not to love again, or certainly not to love deeply, is a tragic one. It often means that, when someone in later life loves them, they cannot let them in. They are no longer emotionally available for love. Alternatively, it means avoiding intimate relationships in later life, or flitting from one relationship to another, to avoid the anticipated hurt of really trusting someone with their love. Loving is far too dangerous. It surely means the pain of rejection and loss. Often such people delude themselves that they do not have a damaged capacity to love. They just keep 'finding good reasons' why staying with X is not right, or why it would never work with Y. Hence they leave a trail of broken hearts, just as once, a long time ago in their childhood, someone broke their heart.

Blowing Myself Up On You

I can't stop blowing myself up on you
I who am skinless from loving you too much,
And so your missile-words fall into my opened self.
Then like a snail, who saw the garden path as safe and good,
In that one instant, loses its home its life its everything,
Guts all splattered on your shoe.

And whilst I'm screaming underfoot,
You snap the little sparrow's neck
Then holding its pleading eyeball in your hand,
Ask what all the fuss is about.
And I do not think you know, do you?
How your smileless good-bye-face,
Reduced me to a rubbish-thing
Who scuttled around in the bits of itself,
Not able to find the light you took with you
When you left.

Margot Sunderland

'Don't care. Don't care. Don't care.' - for a very hurt child, not needing someone at all is so much easier than needing them too much

A girl aged eight, whose father left her said, 'It hurts too much to feel sad.' The helpless state of feeling too much about someone, of desperately needing them or loving them, when they have hurt you deeply, is extremely painful. It is entirely understandable that such children may kill off their love and their need and present themselves to the world as big and tough.

The problem is that cutting off their need and love for Mummy or Daddy often results in cutting off their need for *anyone*. The specific painful interactions they have had with their desperately needed Daddy or Mummy are generalised to all people: 'If you need someone, they will only end up hurting you. So I'll just not need anyone any more. That's the best solution. I'll just look after myself now.' Thus, in many cases, a child's repeated protestation of 'I don't care', of an apparent indifference, is a big defence against the pain of having once cared too much.

A comparison of a child who has cut off from his need with one who has not

> **A child has who cut off from his need for his mother**
>
> David was three. On many occasions his mother hit him. She was overwhelmed by financial worries and had five children to look after. David never cried for his Mummy. He loved his train set and his bike. When his Mummy left him with his Uncle for a month, David did not cry once. When David went to school, he became a bully.

> **A child who has not cut off from her need for her mother**
>
> A little girl aged about three was howling 'Mummy, Mummy!' very loudly down the High Street as her Mummy, obviously very cross with her, was steaming way ahead without once looking back. The little girl's cry was such a terrible cry of desperation and abandonment that many adults stopped in their tracks. Probably the little girl's cries had evoked in some of them a feeling they had once known only too well – an absolute need and yearning for their Mummy. This little girl had not cut off her need for her Mummy, so she clearly endured at times such as these, the terrible pain and desperation of needing a Mummy so badly, while at the same time feeling she has lost her mother's love.

Like it or not, every child needs their Mummy (or equivalent primary caretaker). As Armstrong-Perlman (1992) says, 'A need for his parent is unconditional, in that whatever Mummy does or does not do, the infant still needs her, however much he tells himself that he does not. A child's *love* for his Mummy, on the other hand, is conditional.' Mummy can repeatedly hit him, or be too frightening, or angry with him, and he will stop loving her, but he will not stop needing her. Here lies a mistake that many parents make: they assume that the child's love is unconditional, like their need.

Research shows that children can exhibit signs of emotional detachment from either parent, from as early as three to six months of age (Randolph, 1994, p3). Similarly, one study, 'The Strange Situation Test' (Ainsworth *et al*, 1978), showed that some one-year-olds who had a very anguished relationship with their mother had already moved into a position of false independence. These children are technically known as 'avoidant attached'. Being 'avoidant attached' means hardening your heart with a great deal of pain underneath, and appearing not to need your Mummy, when in fact you need her very badly indeed. In the test, when Mummy left the room, these avoidant attached children just carried on playing. But when the rate of their heartbeats were measured, they were pounding just as furiously as the 'secure attached' children who showed much healthy distress (developmentally speaking) when Mummy went out of the room.

Some children who have been badly hurt in their state of need come to believe that it is far preferable to relate to objects than to people. Objects feel far safer. A computer game, for example, will not hurt you or leave you, yet it can offer a sense of companionship, connection and engagement. One boy aged six, for example, was referred to therapy because, when his mother had baby boy twins, he cut himself off from her and started hugging television sets. Without therapy, many such children who have been too hurt in states of intense infantile need grow up into adults who are frightened of close relationships. Quite simply they are frightened of needing someone ever again.

> When fear commands the mind then the heart is imprisoned.
> (Brian Keenan, 1992, p147)

Children who have hardened their hearts because they think they have lost their parent's love to someone else

My Daddy thinks the new baby is best. (Gary, aged 7)

Sibling

The other, cosied in your breast
You clutching him, your little one
And he will know no dark
With you so constant over him,
Whilst I who have no home in you
But looking on,
To sense your kisses on his brow
And watch him drink his fill of you.
Such taste of sweet and drowsy bliss
Which fills the air with gentle yawn,
His sleep of flesh
All wrapped in you.

These wrong gods
Who chose the other over me,
Granted me not a place in you
And proffered this too vile a toll
To use my tortured eyes
To fix upon your paradise with him,
Weep silent tears, from this too cruel a scene
To see your smiles and tender arms about his little flesh.

Margot Sunderland

Some broken-hearted children become hard and tough because they are convinced that they are the 'unpreferred', the 'unchosen'. Sometimes they are right, sometimes they are wrong. Some suffer the agony of being on the outside of a lyrical couple, and yet looking in. The lyrical couple can be: parent with parent, sibling with parent (such as Mummy with elder sister) or parent with parent's lover. Some children feel doomed to observe this 'lyrical couple' day in, day out throughout their babyhood and/or childhood, having to witness the love, desire and excitement they so desperately want for themselves, going to someone else. 'They use their eyes to drink in somebody else's Garden of Eden' (Armstrong-Perlman, 1995, personal communication).

They experience the established loving couple as a tight unit that makes no overtures to include them. Some children suffering in this way feel erased or wiped out by the perceived or actual favoured other.

Sometimes a child will fight for a place in his parent's heart or mind, pushing into the couple when they are being close, perhaps trying to pushing a sibling off his parent's lap. One little boy would throw things at the bed whenever his mother was sleeping with her new partner. Other children do not protest in this way. They are too defeated. They no longer make overtures towards the parent who they see as having betrayed them. They just harden their hearts instead.

Some children feel too much pain at watching love they once got, now going to someone else. It is true, some mothers do cease to love their older children when the new baby is born, and they have to work to get their loving feelings back. At other times it is pure fantasy on the child's part; Mummy has not gone off him at all. Perhaps she has just not been careful enough to give him sufficient proofs of love at these critical times.

> The phantasies that a child has are of two people who stop him from getting what he wants and demands, but who also point out that they have what he wants, and furthermore are giving it to each other and not to him. (Weininger, 1993, p123)

But, whether fantasy or reality, the rival is perceived as having all the emotional supplies of love, care and goodness. This is often 'understood' by the child in terms of his own worthlessness or inferiority: 'Of course he is preferred to me. He's so clever, attractive and exciting and I am just a blob'; 'I have nothing to give, and she has everything to give'; 'I am nothing. He is everything.' One little boy, aged seven when his baby brother came along, felt that his mother's love for him had died. Powerfully communicating his pain he said, 'I want to die. But I think I am already dead and that the world is already dead.'

Many people make the mistake of thinking that rivalry with a sibling or parent is just a case of competitive feelings, a sense of what is 'not fair', and of envy. For some children it is. For others, it is far, far stronger and far more painful. It is an expression of agonising grief, often coupled with an agonising humiliation of 'having to watch' and an agonising impotence in love. It is not about competition, it is about defeat.

As children are so dependent and their love for their parent by and large is so fiercely loyal, their feelings of betrayal can be all the stronger. They cannot just pick up their dignity and walk out and find another Daddy or Mummy. It is this agony that, for many children, feels unendurable and so they move into the safe retreat of 'I really don't care' and 'Who wants all that soppy love stuff anyway?' They harden their hearts. In fact some children successfully repress their feelings of sibling agony and harden their hearts against the pain for years, only for it to surface with intensity in their adult intimate relationships. This can lead to outbursts of rage from feelings of sexual jealousy. One woman with this childhood history lashed out at her husband because she felt he was more interested in his best male friend than in her. She said, 'It felt strangely like I had to get rid of anything or anyone that got between us. I just lost it.' In some circumstances, when people with a childhood history of betrayal in love find that their partner has been having an affair, their rage escalates to grievous bodily harm, or even to killing their partners because they have felt so erased, annihilated or wiped out by their perceived rival in childhood, and now all these feelings are being unbearably re-triggered.

Children who harden their hearts because someone they desperately loved and needed died, left or was away too long

It is now well established that rupture or loss of a relationship can all too easily lead to violence (see De Zulueta, 1993, p291). For a child, the shock, torment and intense grief of losing one of the most important people in his life can feel like a violent attack – an assault on his very self – coupled, of course, with feelings of aloneness, abandonment, longing and yearning. The 'assault of the loss' can feel as though all his hope, his trust, his love, his whole world have crash-landed: 'he loved her with all of him . . . and then she left. He trusted that s/he would always be there and now she has gone.'

A child who gets no help with these too difficult feelings will often cut himself off from them, repress them or numb himself against them in some other way. However, the 'leaking' from his unconscious often shows itself in some kind of anti-social behaviour such as bullying. Three weeks after his father walked out, Sam, aged eight, said, 'I was sad when Daddy left, but I am normal now.' However, in hardening his heart against his unbearable feelings, Sam is often still haunted by the rage and anger at the 'attack' of the rupture. He hits other children in the playground. For some children, so deep and agonising is this sense of attack that, like Sam, they lash out in protest. When Mummy or

Daddy has gone, they are not there to receive their child's anger or rage, so the attack has to be on somebody else. That way, the absent Mummy or Daddy in their mind can stay good, and the child can maintain some sense of goodness about the world.

A break in a primary relationship can also cause massive disruptions in the brain, psychobiochemically. Too high levels of stress hormone (cortisol) can be released into the blood which easily trigger in a child very primitive reactions of fight or flight. Pert, in her book *Molecules of Emotion* (1997, p271), reports a study in which motherless baby monkeys were fed but not touched or cuddled. They showed symptoms of trauma and depression, and had very high levels of cortisol in their blood. But when an older 'monkey hug therapist' was brought in, who cuddled them, their cortisol levels dropped dramatically. They were no longer in an emergency state of fight or flight.

Harlow and Mears (1979) also studied monkeys who had been separated from their mothers for long periods when they were babies. They then studied how these motherless mothers were with their own babies. The answer was simply horrifically violent:

> Very soon we discovered we had created a new animal – the monkey mother-less mother. These monkey mothers that had never experienced love of any kind were devoid of love for their infants, a lack of feeling unfortunately shared by all too many human counterparts . . . Most of the monkey mother-less mothers ignored their infants, but other motherless mothers abused their babies by crushing the infant's face to the floor, chewing off the infant's feet and fingers, and in one case by putting the infant's head in her mouth and crushing it like an eggshell. Not even in our most devious dreams could we have designed a surrogate as evil as these real monkey mothers. (Harlow & Mears, 1979, p289)

There are many other animal studies showing violence resulting from broken attachment in childhood (see the excellent publication by De Zulueta, 1993).

And now to humans. In the 1950s and 1960s a pair of psychologists, the Robertsons, at The Tavistock Centre in London, made some famous films to show the effects of separating infants from their mothers. They studied infants who had been put in residential nurseries while their mothers were in hospital having a baby. The films showed the marked psychological deterioration of these children, who so clearly moved through the stages of *protest* to *despair* to *detachment* (Bowlby, 1978). Detachment (hardening your heart) happens because the agony of the grief, the desperate longing and yearning, is simply too awful to continue feeling. (If a young child is separated from his mother for too long, he cannot understand that Mummy has not gone forever.) So his too painful feelings are replaced by a hardened heart and a very fragile-built sense of independence: 'I have no need of you. I'll hold myself together now'; 'I'll be the one in control now'; 'No one can hurt me any more.' But such children are still left with the assault of the loss, and so can all too easily move into anger or hate, as a protective armour.

The Robertsons made a film of a one-year-old boy called John who was left for nine days in a residential nursery while his mother had a baby. He was studied again when he was six. The comments are as follows:

> He was still tense and anxious. In particular he seemed unsure of his mother's love for him, and had unprovoked bouts of hostility against her. He himself was puzzled by this, and on one occasion said sadly, 'Why am I so nasty to you Mummy? (Robertson & Robertson, 1969)

John's mother had been extremely loving to him, both before and after the separation. However, the experience of being separated from his mother for just over a week had left him angry with her for years. 'John' and other similar films are still available to the public. (A list of films on mother/child separation is available from the Concord Films Council, 201 Felixstowe Road, Ipswich, Suffolk IP3 9BJ, UK)

The following are stories told by children who became bullies after suffering a major loss.

Neil, aged six

Neil was often excluded from school because of his aggressive behaviour towards other children. Neil's mother had died. Neil had never mourned her. It was too painful. His father was a man married to his work, not his family. Neil's desperate lashing out from a place of unbearable emotional starvation comes out in his story:

'It's a story about Mr Big-as-a-Hill. Both his parents have died. He's OK about that, because he can live on his own. Mr Big-as-a-Hill smashes up the world. He feels very powerful. But Mr Big-as-a-Hill doesn't have nothing to eat. Someone offers him a hamburger but that's not enough. It's never enough. He goes to the jungle and eats whole lions and whole tigers and he's still hungry. He goes to the biggest supermarket in the world and eats all the Mars bars and apple pies and the fish fingers and he's still hungry. Whatever he does he can't make the hunger go away. The hunger is worst at night just before he goes to sleep. So he smashes up the bed and then the bedroom and then the house and then the street and then the whole world.' (Neil's mother used to tuck him up in bed and cuddle him and tell him stories just before he went to sleep.)

In another session, Neil said, 'I think babies cry a lot because they are hungry.'

Sally, aged six

Sally's father, whom she loved very much, just walked out one day. She had never mourned him. She became cold and hard and started bullying. In her play she was always building forts. 'I'm good at keeping people out' she would say repeatedly.

Like Bipley, she was using the forts to guard against anyone else hurting her. The main theme in her stories was that of trying to keep something out. As she eventually melted in her therapy sessions and began to mourn, it became clear that a major part of what she had been trying to keep out (from her own conscious awareness), was lakes and lakes of her own grief.

Sarah, aged twelve

Sarah's mother could not cope with her, so she was put into care. Sarah hardened her heart and regularly smashed up furniture in her care home. She splattered her anger and rage over everyone and everything. Sometimes she would throw fire extinguishers through windows.

Six months into therapy, Sarah's heart began to melt, and she was able to express her grief and desperation underneath all her anger. In play she had repeatedly fed her mother (represented by a little doll) to a two-headed monster. But one day in therapy, she got the monster to regurgitate her mother, and held the doll-mother in her lap, sobbing and sobbing. The picture of her sandplay world (see Figure 4) shows Sarah's despair at being separated from her Mummy, and her feelings of hopelessness at ever being able to get back to her. The picture, in which the way back to Mummy is paved with awful monsters and attacking figures, reminded me of the high, bramble-covered walls in *Sleeping Beauty* which the prince, fuelled by his love, climbed over to reach his princess. Tragically, unlike Sleeping Beauty, this little girl had no such 'proof of love' from her mother.

Figure 4 Sleeping Beauty

Why children who have been too hurt in love or need often turn to a life of anger, hate or bullying

> How will you harden your heart
> To kill [your children]? Is it all steel?
> Before them, will no tear start
> From your eye?
> (Chorus to Medea, *Euripides*, 1994, p32)
>
> Since the joy of loving seems hopelessly barred to him, he may as well deliver himself over to the joy of hating and obtain what satisfaction he can out of that. (Fairbairn, 1952, p27)

When love or need becomes traumatically threatened, it is then that so many children move into a hating or angry response to life. Jason, aged six, said, 'When I feel sad, I go outside and break something.' It is what Guntrip calls 'love made angry', as opposed to 'love made hungry' (1952, p24). The latter also is traumatically-threatened love, but results in a child being desperate for love and attention, as opposed to hardening his heart.

So how exactly does pain in love turn into hate or anger? First, some feelings evoke in a child such a sense of threat that they must be replaced quickly by other, easier feelings. Anger is often that easier feeling. So, for example, when feeling heart-broken, Bipley bullies. This means that in time, he does not need to feel his hurt feelings any more because he tells himself that he is angry, not hurt. Like an effective drug, the anger, for a while at least, makes his hurt go away. For many children, it is far easier to feel angry when hurt, or when desperately grieving for or needing someone, than to feel the agonising rawness of profound emotional pain. Anger can make you feel 'gathered together', potent, strong and mobilised, whereas staying open to your feelings of yearning, hurt, rejection and assumed unloveabililty can make you feel in pieces, unbearably helpless, impotent or ripped apart by your level of pain.

Tragically, however, being perpetually angry or aggressive cuts out most possibilities of a compassionate response. Very few people look at angry children and feel moved, or think 'How tragic, something has gone terribly wrong here for this child.' So the cold responses that these angry children provoke often just strengthen their defences. As we see so often in the classroom, the most closed off children, many of whom are trying to find a way out of their grief or hurt by moving into aggression and anger, are the ones who get into trouble. Tragically, a child who is being big and tough and angry in a classroom of 30 children is a million miles away from being able to say, 'I feel so desperately hurt. I think my Mummy likes my little baby brother far more than me', or 'I see Daddy beat up Mummy. It is unbearable to witness.' So instead of getting understanding and sympathy, they get punished. Philip, aged nine, in a therapy session said, 'I think I just wanted my Mummy to give me a hug. But instead of asking, I hit her. I don't know what made me do it.'

Second, with the realisation of 'I just can't get her to love me' or 'I just can't get her to know how desperate is my need,' the child can feel so impotent that he moves into wanting to attack and destroy, just as he himself feels attacked or destroyed by the intense pain of his impotence in love or need. This pain can make a child lash out at others like a wounded, yelping animal.

> The sadistic person is sadistic because he is suffering from an impotence of the heart, from the incapacity to move the other, to make him respond, to make himself a loved person. He compensates for that impotence with the passion to have power over others. (Fromm, 1973, p263)

Many children who become bullies have at one time felt so attacked by their own level of need that they then cannot bear to see neediness in others. If they do see it, they attack it. They want to wipe it out. Hence the bully who attacks the little child in the playground who is crying for his Mummy. As he attacks the show of neediness in the other, he is often enacting what he himself has once suffered at times when his own neediness met with a shaming, rejecting or angry response.

On meeting too many rejecting responses, some children also start to actively hate the person whom they have needed too much, or rather disown and displace that hate on to some innocent other, in the sense that Schoenewolf describes: 'To hate somebody is to express an intense need for them that has been frustrated' (1991, p14). By and large, hurt can only stay as hurt if the person who has hurt you can really hear, know and understand that they have hurt you. Hurt turns into hate when the person who has hurt you cannot listen, understand, or accept that they have hurt you.

So, in some cases of bullying, the bullied victim is getting all the child's now hateful feelings towards the non-responsive or rejecting parent. It is far easier and safer to attack some weak, small or 'unimportant' child in the playground than to attack your parent, who may love you even less if you do. In cases such as these, bullying is a kind of desperate evacuation process of awful feelings from the too hurt child into another child, rather like using them as a toilet. By this evacuation process, the bully gets his victim to feel helpless and impotent as he himself has felt. Hence bullying is so often also an act of communication.

Children who have hardened their hearts because they have felt betrayed in love can get very angry with their perceived rivals. They may lash out in pain. Being directly angry with his parent may jeopardise the little love a child feels he does have, so he attacks his siblings or displaces his anger onto children in the playground. For example, Tom, aged six, was heart-broken because his mother was clearly besotted with his new baby sister. At school, he kept hitting little girls on the head and kicking female teachers 'for no apparent reason'. He could not stay with feeling broken hearted. He just moved into anger instead. Sometimes a child will lash out from a position (out of their conscious awareness) of, 'If I don't attack him [my brother or sister or some innocent child in the playground] I will be destroyed by the level of this pain inside me, which feels unendurable.' He lashes out at his rival like a wounded animal, desperately trying to protect himself and his 'territory', in the hope that both his rival (the obstacle to his so loved Mummy) and his awful pain will be got rid of.

> And from that torment I will free myself,
> Or hew my way out with a bloody axe.
> (Shakespeare, *Henry VI*, Part 3 III, 2, v,180)

In stories by children who have become bullies because they have felt betrayed in love (have lost their parent's love to another), a very common theme is that of two people fighting over treasure, a jewel, or something else that is very precious. Often the main character in the story feels stolen from and ends up losing something very precious.

Tony, aged nine

Dad left when Tony was five, so there was just Tony and his mother for a while. Then Mum got a new boyfriend. Tony was fine before this, but now he bullies and beats up boys in the playground.

Story one: 'There is this hundred-foot tall King [just like Bipley's feeling of power to cover up not feeling powerful at all], But what nobody knows is that the King is sad. The King robs the green goblin, because the goblin has so much, but as soon as he takes the jewels, they turn to sand in his hand.'

Story two: 'A toad and a frog are fighting over a diamond. The toad killed the frog for taking the diamond. But then the toad felt awful about it.'

Tony then drew a picture of a man and a woman and said, 'I'm going to draw myself in the middle of them.'

Sally, aged eight

Sally was a happy child until her baby sister was born – then she started to become hard and tough and to bully little girls. It was true that Sally was a disappointment to her mother.

Story one: 'The mermaid princess [probably her sister] is next to the queen of the sea kingdom [mother] and Cinderella is looking at them from the shore. The queen snuggles up closer to the mermaid princess, but at night Cinderella managed to creep in and steal from the queen's table.' (In telling her story, at one point Sally accidentally called the queen 'Mum'.)

Story two: 'The Mummy horse and her baby are good, but they are always getting bitten and dead.'

Story three : 'The burglar came and stole the beautiful cow and that meant that all the shops had to close down and shut their shutters because it was too sad. So no-one could buy any milk any more.'

Tracey, aged nine

Tracey was convinced that Daddy loved her little brother and did not like her. She would often stand and watch as her father rocked the new baby on his knee. Tracey became very angry at school. She could not bear her friends to have other friends.

In her story with a doll's house, Tracey put Daddy on a sofa with her little brother. She placed herself separate from them. She then poured brown paint all over her Daddy and her little brother.

Joe, aged seven

Joe was suspended from school because he hit a little girl. Joe felt deeply betrayed by his mother's affection for his new baby sister.

In Joe's stories, 'The snotty baby' always dies. A pig told the cat that he was going to 'kill her kittens.' (At home his mother had referred to him on several occasions as a 'selfish pig'.)

Children who have hardened their hearts because they failed to evoke a positive response in someone who really mattered

All children want to feel that they can evoke responses of delight, love, enjoyment, pride, of 'Wow! What a wonderful sandcastle you've made' or 'That's the best Play-Doh® pizza I have ever seen!' In essence, they want to feel they can light up the adults who are most central in their world. When they fail to get such responses, they do not say, 'Mummy, could you give me more praise for the painting I have brought you as a love gift' or 'Mummy, please show me how much you are delighted with me.' Rather, they just harden their hearts and make the decision, 'Stuff this! I don't *care* any more about getting my Mummy to like what I do.' And they start to build hard, tough defences against all the failed responses they receive, so that they do not have to feel that awful disappointment or let-down any more.

But there is a problem with this particular emotional cutting-off, which is that there is a basic human need to have an effect on others; to be seen; to make our mark on the world. It is a need that, however much we tell ourselves we do not have it, simply does not go away. It runs too deep. It is too central to our make-up. To have any self-esteem, we all have to feel that we can make an impact. In other words, when I have an effect, I know I am somebody, rather than nobody. So if I have no effect, I can easily feel I do not exist at all. Such annihilation anxiety is one of the deepest psychological pains known to human beings.

So children who believe that they cannot have an effect on Mummy or teacher, positively and creatively, settle for a negative effect, and so evoke angry or punishing responses. A destructive or antisocial act is at least ensuring a response.

It is well established that many children who evoke negative attention do so because they have failed to get enough positive, interested or loving attention. Destructive or delinquent acts help a child regain a feeling of potency, 'If I can damage something or somebody, I can see that I can have an effect and therefore I feel I exist. I am somebody.'; 'If I cannot evoke love or warmth in you for me, I can at least evoke fear or hate in you for me. I can at least have that effect.'

Sue Jenner at The Maudesley Hospital in London has developed an extremely innovative and effective therapy called the Parent-Child Game (Jenner, 1999). It is for children who are experienced by their parents as out of control. The parent(s) are observed playing with their child. Jenner repeatedly found that the way the parents were interacting with their child was not giving him any sense of being really enjoyed, of being able to evoke a positive response, or of being able to create something really good. (This was often because these parents had not experienced warm, affirmative responses from their own parents.)

Instead of following the child in his play, noticing and commenting with interest on what he was doing, these parents would issue commands and criticisms, saying something like 'Do this. Put that there. No, not like that.' Or they would just sit silently with the child and show no interest in what he was doing. They would not encourage or praise or say, 'Wow! that looks great', but rather criticise or tell the child that something was not quite right in what he was doing.

When these parents were then enabled to play with their child in ways where the child led the play, where they praised rather than criticised, where they showed real interest in what the child was doing, and where this was part of a wider behaviour modification programme, the child's bad behaviour stopped. In fact, one study showed that there was a 75 per cent decrease in delinquency in disturbed, disruptive children who had undergone the Parent-Child Game when they reached adolescence.

In one parent-child session, it was clear that a six-year-old boy had tried to harden his heart against the pain of his mother's non-responsiveness. He had moved into very destructive behaviour at home and at school. To begin with, he just played with the toys in the room with his mother present. He did not look at her or speak to her once. His manner reminded me of a very depressed adult. But as he was just six, the cement (or, as in the *Bipley* story, the tough stuff) around his heart had not quite set. So when his mother, who did love him (but had to be shown ways to express it) said to him, 'Wow, what a super Play-Doh® pie', he turned to her with utter astonishment and grinned from ear to ear. And in a later session when she said, 'I really like playing with you', he turned to her and gave her a hug and said, 'I love you, Mummy.' This little boy who had been referred because he was so hard and tough was starting to melt.

Chidren who harden their hearts because at home or at school they experience mainly power-based interactions

> Human infants . . . are pre-programmed to develop in a socially co-operative way; whether they do so or not turns in high degree on how they are treated. (Bowlby, 1988, p9)

In some families the main modes of relating, the moment-to-moment interactions, are power-based or control-based as opposed to affection-based: for example, commands, put-downs, blame, criticisms, 'Do this, don't do that'; 'Stop doing that'; 'You stupid little fool'; 'Don't'. 'Stop whinging, otherwise I'll give you something to whinge about.'

Children from such family backgrounds have all too little knowledge of ways of relating that are about 'power *with* another', as opposed to 'power *over* another'. The former interactions involve a sense of 'let's . . . ' and 'you and me together' and 'us co-operating', rather than 'us locked in a power struggle'. They involve feeling 'we can make this lovely thing together' or 'we share this lovely thing with each other' or 'we can just enjoy being together.'

In an environment where there are too many power-based and control-based interactions, it really is not safe to express warm or tender feelings – to have an open heart. It would be foolhardy to stay soft in such a harsh environment where by and large, expression of vulnerable feeling is seen as weakness. So when children from such family cultures feel sad, hurt or broken-hearted they are likely to just bottle it up and over time harden their hearts. A child who has a daily diet of these sorts of power-based or control-based interactions (with no kind aunt or significant compassionate teacher to model a powerful alternative) may simply 'identify with the aggressor'; internalise a harsh inner parent and become like them. There is a lot of truth here in 'If you can't beat 'em, join 'em.'

In fact De Zulueta (1993, p66) discusses how these early modes of submission-dominance relating, can become firmly implanted templates for relationship in a child's mind. This means that such children can then go on through life turning all their relationships into issues of power over (dominance) or power under (submission). This, of course, spoils or destroys any potentially loving relationship, because sooner or later the power-based interactions blight the affection-based interactions. In some relationships these children may be victimised (submission); in others they will dominate and bully.

One marked example of this was a boy of ten from a very power-based background with much physical violence. He said he liked a girl in his class, very, very much. Sadly, however, the only way he could express his affection to her was by hitting her. He had no other model of how to be with people you like; no model of tender, cooperative, loving exchange. His only way of responding to feeling really strong feelings for someone, was to hit them.

It is easy to pick out children in a playground who have a very restricted range of ways of being with another person – that is, only submission-dominance 'relational options'. You can watch these children either bullying or being bullied, according to who they are with. Playground studies (Troy & Sroufe, 1987; Main & George, 1985) have shown that children from such backgrounds show no sympathy if they see other children upset and crying. Children who have not been shown enough empathy themselves for *their* sad feelings tend to try and 'shut up' distressed children in the playground, by verbally or physically attacking them. In contrast, children from a background of warm and kind interactions do show concern, even at the age of one.

If you are a boy, the effect of a harsh family culture can be ten times worse because of gender stereotypes. So boys who have hardened their hearts in this way often pick on other boys who seem to them to be effeminate, open and vulnerable. They attack in the other what they have cut off in themselves. Trauma theorists (Van der Kolk, 1989; De Zulueta, 1993) would argue that this is an out-of-awareness acting out of how these aspects have been attacked in themselves.

Stories enacted or told by children from submission-dominance backgrounds who bully and/or behave destructively, include the following:

Hattie, aged 10

Hattie was so controlling and bossy that no-one wanted to be her friend. Her teachers said they found both her parents frightening. In therapy, Hattie repeatedly enacted stories about people fighting incessantly, and yet she also managed to convey how this made her feel very fragmented. (In Figure 5, note the fragmented figure in the middle of all the attacking images.)

On numerous occasions, Hattie also tried to get her therapist to role-play stories of submission-dominance: 'I want to throw you in prison'; 'You've got to punish me'; 'You be a little worm and then I'll tread on you'; 'You be someone who shouts at me. It makes me happy.'

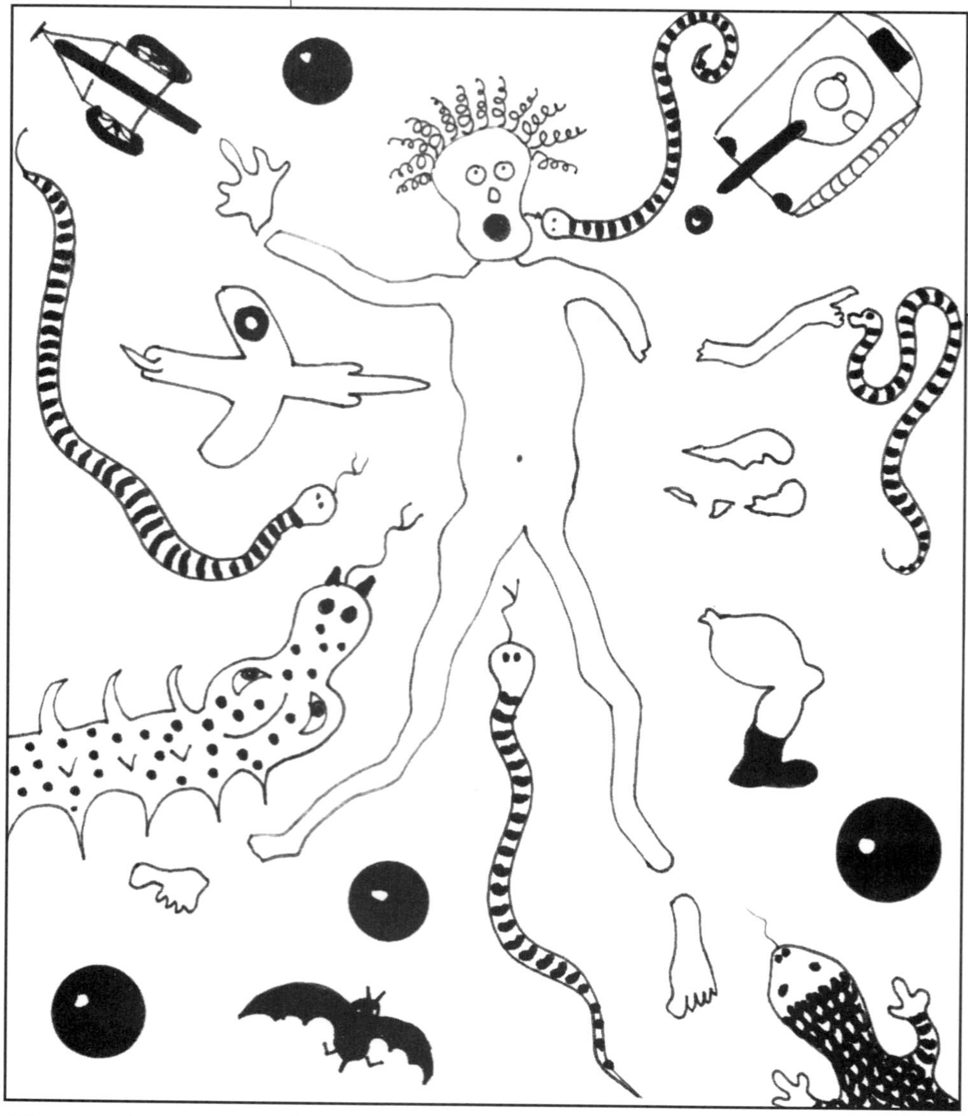

Figure 5 Drawing of Hattie's sandplay

Gerry, aged eight

Gerry had a father who was always exploding into fits of rage and blame. At school, Gerry locked people out of rooms, flooded washbasins and regularly set off the fire alarm. He seemed to feel no guilt about it whatsoever. His stories included the following:

'A monster trod all over the little boy.'

'A tiger trod on a butterfly, just because it wanted to. And the little butterfly said, 'Please don't let me die', but the tiger just roared at it more.'

Sophie, aged nine

Sophie's mother had a string of very abusive relationships. The police were often called in. Sophie attacked other children rather than playing with them. She had no friends.

Story one: 'The Mummy in the story keeps touching fireworks. They keep blowing her up and killing her.'

Story two: 'A girl dies. The brothers poo on the dead girl's grave, and stamp on it and sick on it.' On relating this story, Sophie said 'It's good isn't it, there is no violence in my story today.' (I think she saw violence as just people getting hit)

Story three: 'Monsters are swimming with the children in the swimming pool. Just when you think it's all right, that's when they attack.'

Ned, aged six

Ned was regularly hit by both his parents. He was suspended from school on several occasions for violent outbursts. His stories were full of breaking, crashing and smashing. He said to his therapist: 'If I can't break something I don't want to play with you', and 'If I can't do crashing, there is no point in coming to you any more.'

Children who bully because they have felt unbearably powerless in some form of trauma

Every persecutor was once a victim. (Miller, 1987, p249)

Children who have suffered traumatic powerlessness, such as in watching Daddy hit Mummy, or Mummy leave Daddy, or from having suffered sexual or physical abuse, may harden their hearts and banish their powerless feelings to the dark basement of their unconscious. This defence is called repression, which can be described as forgetting that you have forgotten something.

Trauma research has shown that, if a trauma of unbearable powerlessness and helplessness is repressed, it is often unconsciously acted out, but this time by making someone else feel the powerless, helpless feelings the victim himself has suffered. With repression, because these feelings are so completely disowned, it is this that also makes them so likely to be *projected* on to someone else. Other people seen as 'weak and helpless' are then often despised, or actually attacked, emotionally or physically. The unconscious logic often runs something like this: 'I don't need to feel my own fear if I make someone else feel scared instead.' 'I can avoid feeling impotent by making someone else feel a helpless victim.' 'If they feel my feelings, I don't have to have them any more.'

This defence mechanism of projecting feelings of helplessness on to others is also one of the reasons why some parents verbally or physically attack their children, often very brutally, and why some even kill their children.

As in previous years, children under one year were the most likely to be victims of homicide for offences recorded during 1994. (Home Office, 1994, p74)

They cannot bear to see in their children the helplessness and powerlessness that they have killed off as too dangerous in themselves. For some parents, the helpless child becomes an intolerable reminder of their own pain, and so must be attacked. 'All reminders of inner weakness or of pain must be banished, even at the cost of the self or dehumanisation of the "other" ' (De Zulueta, 1993, p276). The recent massacres of children in school playgrounds in Dunblane and Wolverhampton, and in the United States can also be seen in this light.

It is vital that more teachers realise that much bullying *is an enactment of a trauma,* and a communication about what the bully himself has suffered.

Therefore many bullies need professional help. They are not bad, they are simply suffering from a post-traumatic haunting. It is usually only if a child is fortunate enough to go to counselling or therapy that the unconscious communication about his trauma is met and understood, brought to his conscious mind and so fully felt. It is often only then that the unconscious acting-out of the trauma can stop for good.

Give Us

Give us something to destroy:
A corolla, a silent corner,
A boon companion, a magistrate,
A telephone booth,
A journalist, a renegade,
A fan of the opposing team,
A lamp-post, a man-hole cover, a bench.
Give us something to deface:
A plaster wall, the Mona Lisa,
A mudguard, a tombstone.
Give us something to rape:
A timid girl,
A flower-bed, ourselves.
Don't despise us; we're heralds and prophets.
Give us something that burns, offends, cuts, smashes, fouls,
And makes us feel that we exist.
Give us a club or a Nagant,
Give us a syringe or a Suzuki.
Pity us.

Primo Levi

Children who have hardened their hearts because they have been shamed

Some shaming is verbal, such as vicious put-downs, whereas some can be physical, like being smacked with one's pants down. Sometimes it is done entirely through a killing look. Sometimes the adult does not actively shame the child, but the child feels shamed, for example if he is expressing his love for his mother and she turns away, or if she refuses or shows indifference to his love gift, or if he tells her about something he is very proud of and she belittles it.

Shame is a lethal emotion. Hence it is sometimes referred to as 'killing shame'. If it gets through, it is often experienced as a major assault on the self, on one's very personhood. Shaming a child makes him feel that the whole of him is not OK – not just his behaviour, but his very being. When a child hardens his heart because he has been traumatically shamed he usually does one of three things:

1   Retreats 'into his shell'. This is a contracted, stifled response to the world, devoid of any spontaneity, creativity or expansiveness. The problem is that this can become a way of being.

2   Moves into what Mollon calls 'countershame' – 'a kind of manic denial of shame in which [he] behaves as if he . . . has no experience of shame' (Mollon, 1993, pp44–45).

3   Moves into shaming others (shame-rage, see below).

With 2 and 3 a child can move into doing what has been done to him, move into shaming, ridiculing or humiliating others. For example, Ben, aged seven, had been brutally shamed by his father. At playtime, Ben would go around saying to the most vulnerable, innocent-looking children, things like 'Your mother is a whore', or 'cretin', 'slag', 'poofter', 'you're mental'. His victims would often burst into tears, a human response that Ben no longer allowed himself.

Shaming not only evokes feelings of utter worthlessness (which are often, as we have seen, repressed and projected) , but there it can also lead to a seething build-up of feelings of rage. This is known as 'shame-rage', and it is a natural reaction to such a brutal attack as being shamed. As a child, Hitler was shamed every day:

> Unable to leave, he must put up with everything; not until he has grown up can he take any action. When Hitler was grown and came to power, he was finally able to avenge himself a thousandfold . . . for his own misfortune. (Miller, 1987, p196)

Also many murderers who were shamed and humiliated as children have felt compelled to torture their victims before killing them, as Jurgen Bartsch did:

> With great excitement he repeatedly went through the motions of destroying himself in his victims – now he is no longer the helpless victim but the mighty persecutor!' (Miller, 1987, p224)

Children who harden their hearts because they have been hit repeatedly

In my many years of work as a child therapist, I have found a recurring and disturbing theme in the play of a great many children who have been regularly, and often severely, beaten by their parents. In their stories they say something along the lines of the following:

'Mummy is dead.'; 'I have no Daddy.'; 'My Mummy is dead – No, not really.' or 'My Dad died yesterday. He didn't really.' In a sense it is true. If a child is repeatedly hit by his mother, he has a mother but not a Mummy. If he is repeatedly hit by his father, he has a father, but not a Daddy. Mummies and Daddies are people to whom you turn for protection, *not people you need to be protected from*. Mummies and Daddies are fundamentally warm and kind (even if they do sometimes lose their tempers).

Some children harden their hearts because they feel betrayed by a parent who repeatedly hits them. Each time they are hit, the nails in the coffin of their relationship with that parent go deeper. Bit by bit they move into a bitter place. The tragedy is that many parents do not realise that they can all too easily kill off their child's love for them. They think the blood-tie means an automatic love. How wrong this is. As in the film, *Nil by Mouth*, the husband who regularly beats up his wife in a moment of vulnerability says, 'My father thought the word "father" was enough – It wasn't.'

One day Tommy, aged eight, said to his therapist, 'My mother beats me.' He talked of his mother in cold, hard tones. The therapist was concerned that his mother was actually killing off Tommy's love for her. So, with Tommy's agreement, the therapist asked to see the mother. The mother then realised that her relationship with her son was in jeopardy. She did not want to lose his love. So she and Tommy set out together to mend their broken relationship. The mother said to him how sorry she was. She threw away her hitting stick. As a result, Tommy did not harden his heart against her. But Tommy was eight. With an older child, it can all too easily get past the point of forgiveness.

The following are some of the stories told or enacted by children who have hardened their hearts because they have been hit repeatedly:

Peter, aged five

Peter was hit by his father. He also watched his father hit his little brother and his mother.

'Squirrel and Mummy squirrel are good, but they are always getting eaten and dead.'

'Is there a Daddy in the story?' asked the counsellor. 'Daddy is dead,' said Peter. Peter also told a story about 'A big tree in the garden who spikes the petals of the little flowers.'

Trudi, aged five

Trudi was repeatedly hit by her mother.
'This is a story about three Mummies – one is a smiling Mummy, one is not a real Mummy and the third Mummy is dead.'

Tracy, aged eight

Tracy was often smacked. Her mother drank and shouted a lot. 'In this story there are always volcanoes exploding, bees stinging, and dogs biting.'

'This is a story about The Tower of London. It has bars on the windows in case it gets hit by some passing missile. I've drawn a warning light on the top of it to stop it getting hit.'

Children who harden their hearts because they have witnessed parental violence

Bobby, aged six
My Mum is not kind when she is fighting my Dad.

Gemma, aged seven
I think I locked my fear about it away in a cupboard.

It is both very common and very understandable for children to harden their hearts when they have watched parental violence and no one has helped them with their feelings about it. Just think about the feelings involved: the impotent rage; the agony at seeing someone you love being beaten up by someone else you love; the aloneness of no one coming to help; the terrible helplessness of not being able to stop it happening. As one six year-old said, as he watched his Mummy being beaten up by his Daddy, 'I so wanted to hit him, but I was too little.'

It is quite understandable that you would want to close your heart to all of this, to bury your feelings about it, to get hard and tough. Watching something so horrific, the child has felt too much, so now he must 'put tough stuff' around his heart so that, in future, he can feel very little. In terms of trauma theory, as we have explored above, it is not surprising that many children who have witnessed parental violence then become violent themselves. They enact what they have seen, but often this time with themselves as the persecutor. It is the mind's way of desperately trying to process the event.

Below are stories told by children who have witnessed parental violence, and who after the trauma became big and tough. Some were referred for counselling because they had become bullies. Note how, in so many of the stories, help is rendered impotent. It is a comment through story, on the awful pain of no one coming to help either Mummy or themselves, the watcher.

In all these cases, the children saw their father beat up their mother.

Sally, aged seven

After witnessing parental violence, Sally became extremely aggressive. She has no friends.

'In this story, too many things get broken. Even the Mummy gets broken. So the little girl becomes a bomb, so that no one can break her.'

Lee, aged eight

Lee is withdrawn and a loner.

'The little frog is calling for his mum, 'Mum, Mum, there's a big bad wolf – help me I'm frightened!', but the frog's mum runs away frightened. The policeman tries to come, but he gets stuck in a prickly bush on the way.'

In another story, 'There are wild cats raging and the little girl dies.' When the teacher asked her why the little girl died, Lee said, 'She was too alone with her fears.'

Peter, aged seven

Peter was suspended from school because he punched on the nose a little girl who was crying.

'In this story, Mum is in the house being buried again. The man must be killed. It is a sad and scary story.'

'A pig took away the Daddy's heart so that he did not remember his kindness.'

'A fire engine tries to save but gets destroyed on the way.'

Sam, aged eight

Sam watched a scene in which Daddy was beating her sister. So her mother attacked her father. And then Sam and her brothers tried to get their mother off their father. Now Sam bullies little children, and is very behind in her schoolwork. She trusts no one.

'In this story people are always battling. They are very wounded and bleeding, but they still have to fight. All the policemen are asleep somewhere on a far distant beach in Australia.'

WHAT YOU CAN DO AFTER YOU HAVE READ *A WIBBLE CALLED BIPLEY (AND A FEW HONKS)* TO A CHILD

This section offers ideas for things to say and do after you have read this story to a child. The tasks, games and exercises are designed specifically to help a child to think about, express and further digest his feelings about the story's theme.

As previously discussed, children often cannot speak clearly and fully in everyday language about what they are feeling, but they can show or enact, draw or play out their feelings. Therefore, many of the exercises in this section offer support for creative, imaginative and playful modes of expression. They are also designed to inspire a child to respond further by telling his own stories.

In order that you avoid asking the child too many questions (children can soon feel interrogated), some exercises just require a tick in a box, or the choosing of a word or image from a selection.

Please note The tasks, games and exercises are not designed to be gone through in chronological order. Also, there are far too many to attempt them all in one go – the child could feel bombarded. So just pick the ones you think would be right for the child you are working with, taking into account his age, and how open he is to the subject matter. Instructions to the child are in tinted boxes.

☆ Frozen feelings

Do you think you have some frozen feelings ?

Frozen feelings are the ones that have hurt too much for you to carry on fully feeling them. So you have tried to stop feeling them. They are also the ones that are just too lonely to feel on your own. Put a tick next to any of these feelings below that you think are feelings you have frozen:

Anger ☐

Hurt ☐

Sad ☐

Furious ☐

Disappointed ☐

Broken-hearted ☐

Too lonely ☐

Needing someone too much ☐

Missing someone too much ☐

Feeling not wanted ☐

Too frightened inside ☐

Too wobbly inside ☐

Too much fighting inside ☐

Too let down ☐

Too much 'unfair' ☐

☆ People who have hurt you

- ◉ Draw, make in clay or write down the names of the people who have hurt you the most in your life.

- ◉ What would you like to say to them if they were here now, and if they could really listen and take in what you had to say to them? Write it or say it or, using speech bubbles, draw yourself saying it.

- ◉ How does it feel telling them the things that you have never told them?

☆ Too-horrid things to see

- ◉ Draw or show in sandplay a scene in your life which was so horrid that it meant you had to put 'tough stuff' around your heart, like Bipley.

- ◉ You could imagine it as a scene in a film, so draw or build your film set.

- ◉ What do you feel when you look at the scene now? Is there anything you would like to do to the scene which you couldn't do at the time (such as adding something or taking something away)? If so, do it now. What does it feel like now that you have done it?

☆ Running away from feelings that hurt you too much

- ◎ Have you ever felt so sad, hurt, angry, scared or lonely that you wanted to run away from or cut yourself off from the too awful feeling in some way?

- ◎ Did you manage?

- ◎ If so, how did you do it?

- ◎ What was good about stopping yourself from feeling the feeling?

- ◎ What was bad about stopping yourself from feeling the feeling?

- ◎ To help you think – these are some of the common ways that people try to stop having the painful feelings they are having: eat something; drink something; tidy something; bully someone; tell a lie; hurt someone; watch television; play with their computer; do things very, very quickly, rushing from one thing to another; smash something; break something.

☆ 'Keep out'

In trying to stop people hurting you any more, or making you sad or scared, do you ever feel like any of these? Tick if you do.

A creature with a very hard shell, such as a tortoise, a whelk, an oyster, an aardvark ☐

A knight in armour ☐

A castle or fortress with a deep moat, high walls and a drawbridge ☐

The Great Wall of China (such a huge wall, it can be seen on earth from the moon) ☐

A locked door ☐

A block of ice ☐

A rock ☐

If it is none of these, draw how you think you guard yourself from people hurting you.

☆ The good things and the not-so-good things about being tough

- ◎ If you have had to put invisible armour around your heart like Bipley, because of what has happened to you in your life, what does it feel like?

- ◎ What's good about it?

- ◎ What's bad about it?

- ◎ Is there anything you think you miss out on by being so tough?

- ◎ Draw what you would think would happen to you if you took off your invisible armour and became gentler, calmer or kinder.

☆ Being a hard guy from the movies for a day

Which of these characters would you most like to be if you could be one for a day?

The Incredible Hulk ☐
Darth Vader ☐
A Ninja Turtle ☐
Schwarzenegger ☐
Robocop ☐
Predator ☐
Terminator II ☐
Batman ☐

- ◎ What would you spend your day doing?

- ◎ What would you feel being them?

- ◎ What would you miss about being *you*, if you were them all the time instead of just for one day?

- ◎ What would you not miss about being you, if you were them all the time instead of just for one day?

☆ Walls in stories

There are lots of fairy stories and myths about walls – actual walls that make people unreachable, and emotional walls around people's hearts. Below are some examples. Do you feel that any of the characters are a bit like you and your life? Tick if you do.

Rapunzel, walled up in her tower, away from the world of people ☐

The Snow Queen in her faraway palace of ice ☐

The little boy into whose heart the Snow Queen put some ice ☐

Sleeping Beauty, asleep behind very high walls with lots of brambles, so it is very, very difficult to get to her ☐

The Minotaur, who was put underground because he was so awful ☐

Alice In Wonderland down a hole, and at first she didn't want to be found and then she did ☐

☆ Heart in bits

◎ Has anyone ever broken your heart?

◎ How badly did it get broken?

◎ Draw what your heart felt like before it got broken. Then draw it after it got broken. Or, if you prefer, show this in clay.

◎ Have you done anything to try to mend your heart, as Bipley did when he put tough stuff around his heart? If you have, draw your heart after you have tried to mend it. Has it worked?

☆ 999: Time for tough stuff!

Think of a time this week, when were you hard as if you were wearing tough stuff, like Bipley, around your heart.

- ◎ Why did you need it then?
- ◎ Was there a time this week when you melted some of your toughness and were a softer you?
- ◎ What or who made it safe enough for this to happen?

☆ All about good power and bad power

Good power is about feeling strong because you are doing something with someone, or for someone that makes you and/or them feel better or happier, and that does not hurt anyone else in the process. Batman uses good power. It is called 'power with' someone.

Bad power is called 'power over'. It is when you do something to someone that hurts their body or hurts their feelings, but it makes you feel powerful. Darth Vader uses bad power.

- ◎ Can you think of times in your life when you have used good power?
- ◎ Can you think of times in your life when you have used bad power?
- ◎ Can you think of times when people have used good power or bad power with you?
- ◎ If so, draw or write the times you remember the most.

☆ High walls, low walls or no walls

- ⊚ With whom in your life do you need to have walls or armour so that they cannot hurt you?

- ⊚ With whom in your life do you feel safe enough to be less hard and tough? Draw or write your answer.

- ⊚ With whom in your life do you need a very big wall or very tough armour because they make you feel bad, unhappy or frightened, or because they also have big, tough walls? Draw them and draw you with your armour on or your wall.

- ⊚ Is there anyone in your life who you can dare to be with without any wall or armour at all? That means someone you could cry with, or ask for a hug from or someone to whom you could say, 'I'm scared or lonely or sad,' and you would know they would understand.

- ⊚ Who in your life sees the real you behind your hard tough image?

- ⊚ Who in your life just sees you being big and tough all the time and thinks that this is all you are?

- ⊚ Who in your life do you think would like to see more of you from behind your big and tough walls?

☆ Street cred

What do you fear would happen if you stopped being a tough guy for a while, and told someone that you were sometimes upset, scared, sad, lonely and so on ?

Tick if you believe any of the things below would happen to you, if you told someone of these feelings.

People would hurt me ☐
People would laugh at me ☐
I'd be seen as weak ☐
I'd lose my street cred ☐
I'd get bullied ☐
No one would like me ☐
I'd be called a sissy ☐
Something awful would happen – I don't know what ☐

If it is not any of these – draw what you think might happen.

☆ You in a fortress

◎ Draw a fortress, or make one out of clay.

◎ Now choose miniature people or miniature animals [toys] to stand for the main people in your life. Show which ones you would let into your fort, and which ones you would keep out – and why. Place them inside or outside your fort. You may want to say why you have put them where you have put them.

☆ The place of 'all safe at last'

◎ Draw a place where you would feel really, really safe – a place where no one could ever hurt you, or make you feel too sad, or too frightened, or too hurt ever again.

◎ Would it have any people in it (the ones you really like or feel very safe with)? Draw them in if it would. Or would you be in the place alone?

◎ What would you do there?

☆ Bridges instead of walls

Maybe there is someone in your life who you trust more than most other people, who you could build a bridge towards, rather than a wall?

◎ If there is someone like that, draw yourself on this bridge, and the person you trust waiting for you on the other side. Draw a thought bubble or a speech bubble coming out of your mouth. Write in it what you are thinking or saying.

◎ Draw a thought bubble or a speech bubble coming out of their mouth. Write in it what they are thinking or saying.

◎ How does it feel, having a bridge not a wall?

✰ When something awful happens (for children who have suffered a trauma)

Has anything horrid happened to you, or have you ever seen anything horrid?

Draw what it felt like to be you before this awful thing happened.	
Draw what it felt like to be you while this awful thing was happening.	
Draw what it felt like to be you after this awful thing happened.	

Do you feel bad for not being able to stop what happened from happening?

Do not pressurise the child to tell you what the awful thing is. If the child says he did feel bad for not being able to stop what was happening, it may be relevant and appropriate to say something like, 'You are not bad for not stopping it. You couldn't have stopped it, because you were too little; and children haven't got the thinking in their brain to stop it, or the knowing how to stop it. That's why it is the responsibility of grown-ups, not children, to stop the bad things from happening. When grown-ups were your age, they wouldn't have been able to stop it either.'

☆ Colourful world

> When he was miserable and alone, Bipley's world lost all its colour.
>
> ☺ When has the world been the most colourful for you?
>
> ☺ When has it lost its colour? Draw one or more of these colourless times if you like.

A note on the benefit of working with creative media with children who have hardened their hearts is appropriate at this point. Sandplay, painting, clay and music are excellent modes of expression to communicate the intensity of hating or angry or hurt feelings. In a therapeutic setting, having these modes of expression as resources can enable the child to find alternatives to turning feelings inwards against himself or destructively acting them out on other people. Instead, these feelings can be expressed, processed and heard through creativity and imagination.

What to say to children who are angry, aggressive or who bully

Bullies, in a one-to-one situation with someone they trust and who is there to try to understand rather than criticise, often start to melt. They begin to feel, and are able to think about what they have done to someone and why. Through empathic response, many children can understand and think about many of the things written in this workbook, about why bullies become bullies. Some feel enormous relief at being given this information. Many have just written themselves off as some kind of monster.

Weininger, in his book *Children's Phantasies* (1989), talks of a boy who went around attacking other children mercilessly. The boy calmed down when someone understood how he was trying to get rid of his pain by getting someone else to feel it. 'I think you are trying to hurt everyone else so that the hurt will leave you. If you damage the other kids you may not feel as damaged' (Weininger, 1989, p167).

For children who have become bullies after some kind of trauma, you may wish to explain as follows:

> Sometimes trauma makes you keep repeating, and acting out some of the aspects of what has happened to you. So if, for example, you were bullied, you might bully someone, and get them to feel what you felt. It is your mind trying to come to terms with what has happened to you. But the acting-out can get you into trouble, and spoil your life as well as other people's. So one way to stop this from happening is to talk about what has happened to you or to draw it, or show it in the sandplay. Once you express it in one of these ways, then it is like a ghost that can be put to rest. Without your doing this thinking and feeling about what has happened to you, your past can be like a ghost that haunts you and spoils your life.

Some hard and tough children do not know how they are coming across, or what reaction they are evoking in others. Tom (aged twelve) was obsessed with toy soldiers. As a little boy, he had repeatedly seen his mother hit his father. In other words, he had lived in a war zone. He was often very attacking when anyone said anything to him. He did not understand why people seemed not to like him. One day his therapist explained to him what she saw was happening. As it can be difficult for children to concentrate on things expressed in verbal language only, his therapist enacted what she was saying with little figures. For the child, this is rather like watching a little play.

This is what the therapist both said and enacted through miniature figures:

When you get hurt, or sad, or scared, it's like you become your soldiers and your strong fortress walls, and then people get angry or scared back. But they are not angry or scared of *you* because they can't see *you* behind your strong fortress walls. They are getting cross and scared of your walls. And so they attack you, and that makes you think 'Well, that just proves how much I need my walls and my angry words!' But you see, it's not really you and them fighting. It's *your* army and *your* walls fighting *their* army and *their* walls. So all the delightful fun and the possible lovely things that could happen between you and them can never happen.

The therapist then showed some lovely things happening in the sand-pit, such as two boys enjoying fishing together, a group sitting around a birthday table, and some people making a boating pond together. Tom knew what she meant, because he and his therapist had shared some lovely 'power-with' as opposed to 'power-over' times too.

Tom began to understand how he was provoking hostile responses. So gradually, as the therapy continued, he dared to take down his walls brick by brick. When he did, he found chinks of light coming through. These were in the form of people's kind, affectionate and playful responses to him, instead of their previous aggressive, heavily-defended attacks, when they had to defend themselves against *his* heavily defended attacks.

Finally, it is vital to verbalise your empathy about the child's need to have such strong defences; how you can imagine that some things must have happened to him that have made him not trust people, and need to keep them out. Trying to reach out and form a meaningful connection to a child who lives within a highly defended protective fortress can be very difficult. Kindness and concern can metaphorically fall on the floor between you, never reaching the child. You can only wait and give space and respect for his defences, rather than trying to knock them down. You may, at some stage, explain that, for most of the time, if humans are treated kindly and warmly, they will be kind and warm (like Bipley, before he became a Honk). But if humans have been too hurt or treated unkindly, it is understandable that they will put tough stuff around their hearts as Bipley did, and so become hard and even cruel.

How to help children with their confusion and belief that it is brave not to feel and it is sissy to cry

Surrender is not weakness . . . It is a powerful non-resistance. (Williamson, 1992, p49)

Children often need help in understanding that letting go into feelings often takes far more courage than defending against them. You might say something along the following lines:

Anyone can be big and tough, because it's easy to be big and tough. Anyone can put up a wall, put tough stuff around their heart and decide not to feel. The brave thing is to dare to feel. It takes real strength and courage to dare to feel very strong feelings, because some strong feelings can hurt a lot. It is like daring to take out a little boat on a very strong sea. A lot of children just stay on the shore.

It is important also to tell children how important it is that they do not go out in the little boat on their own. Strong feeling should always be felt in the presence of someone who can understand. (The strong sea refers to the intensity of arousal in very strong feeling, the intensity of emotional pain.)

It is often very helpful to explain to children who bully, or who have hardened their hearts, that it is not weak but strong and brave to show tender feelings. As one thirteen-year-old boy said, in a very moving and insightful moment, 'I don't know if I'm strong enough to be soft.' You might tell them how in war it is the weakest men who do not dare to cry. In this vein, Frankl, talking about the Second World War said: 'Tears bore witness that a man had the greatest of courage, the courage to suffer. Only a few realised that' (1985, p100).

Similarly, Nina Herman, a psychologist, talks about the strength it takes to really mourn the people she had lost after years of defending herself against her grief: 'Until this time they had shared a shadowy mass grave since I had not mourned them individually because I did not have the strength. And so this mourning now began' (1988, p142).

It is also important to talk about the place of appropriate defences 'to protect your heart and close in if you are ever with people who would only jeer or get angry if you showed your sad or hurt feelings'.

How to help a child find (just as Bipley did) less drastic ways to protect himself from hurt

After reading the story, you may find a way of emphasising to the child how the story shows that hardening your heart shuts out all the warmth and the light, and puts the brakes on your development as a person.

Very defended children need help to consider other less drastic forms of defence. They often need to be taught assertiveness and negotiation skills. Also, many children find that having the word 'hurt' in their vocabulary helps: for example, 'I'm hurt by what you said or did' (said to the right person of course – not to another bully). This can then become an alternative to using anger as a response to hurt.

When a child has been helped to have a wider feeling vocabulary, it can often melt the hardest of parents. With the help of his therapist Charlie (aged seven) for example, rather than continuing to steal from his mother's purse, said, 'I feel so hurt and left out when you have the baby on your lap, and that's why I get cross.' His mother had had no idea. This brave and emotionally literate statement on Charlie's part did so much to start the process of mending their broken relationship.

It is important to give the child who has a hardened heart as many delicious, delightful, 'power-with' as opposed to 'power-over' interactions as possible. There is little point in saying to a hardened-hearted child or a bully who only really knows about submission-dominance ways of relating, 'Look! You are missing out on the delights of warm, playful, affectionate relationships.' Such children may have no concept (or only a very faded one) of what you are talking about. The only way to invite them into the pleasures and potentials of human relationship is to give them experiences of lovely interactions, which means doing something which is fun, warm, gentle or creative together. Any activity based on 'let's'; on humour; on funny and non-hurtful physical play is ideal.

But for some very defensive children who have been brought up on a diet of power-based relationships, these new ways of relating can feel uncomfortable and sometimes threatening. They can be experienced as an attack on the child's very belief system about himself, about other people and the world. Some children have become so acclimatised to a harsh world, both inside their head and in their outer world, that they find kindness disturbing. It is just too unfamiliar. As one little boy said to his teacher when she was being very, very kind, 'Look, I'd like it better if you shouted at me.' What he was probably saying was, 'It is disturbing when you are being so different to how I know this harsh and hostile world to be. It throws everything I know about myself and other people up in the air. At least I know where I am with the status quo.'

CONSIDERING FURTHER COUNSELLING OR THERAPY FOR CHILDREN WHO HAVE HARDENED THEIR HEARTS AND/OR BECOME BULLIES

> We can only really mourn in the presence of another. (Bowlby, 1973)

In 1999 in Great Britain, 40 per cent of crime on the streets was committed by boys aged ten to fourteen. The Government's reaction to this was to promise more money to schools for literacy and numeracy for ages four to six. Other politicians from time to time say we should concentrate more on moral education, to reduce the violence and crime in young people.

This reaction to juvenile crime comes from a grossly ignorant position about the latest research in neurobiology and child psychology; trauma theory; the effect of abuse and neglect on the psychobiochemistry of the brain and about how the mind needs to repeat and repeat unworked-through trauma. It fails to take into account how children who have felt unbearably impotent, weak or helpless will often, as a result, attack the weakness and helplessness in others as a communication about how they have felt, or rather to try to get rid of these feelings by passing them on to other people. It fails to consider how, when a child has been terribly emotionally hurt, his heart can harden against that hurt, so that he can no longer feel his own emotional pain, or anybody else's for that matter.

No amount of literacy, numeracy or moral education will stop children like Bipley from becoming bullies. Only someone willing to listen to their pain and their hurt consistently over time, until they start to melt, can do that. Most teachers do not have the time to be with the pain and hurt under every bully's angry acting out. In contrast, a counsellor or therapist has the time to wade through the monster-like tentacles of the seven-year-old little horror (who is on the brink of exclusion from school), to the desperately hurting infant who lies underneath.

The situation is serious. If children who have hardened their hearts do not get one-to-one therapeutic help, the consequences for society continue to look bleak. How many cases of children bullying, abusing, and sometimes even killing other children do we have to endure before this is realised? Without counselling or therapy, children from power-based, submission-dominance family cultures are likely to continue throughout their lives repeating submission-dominance relationships, and so causing all manner of suffering to themselves and others. Some children have been so hurt in love that, without therapy, they may never dare to love again in a deep, enduring sense.

Furthermore, the trouble is that without counselling or therapy, many hardened children do not even allow themselves to know that they are scared, hurt or grieving, so they cannot let anyone else know, and consequently they remain unhelped. Many people think that kindness and warmth are enough to melt children like Bipley. This is often not the case because the child's painful past experiences remain unprocessed. Hence the situation of the child receiving all sorts of loving kindness and yet still beating up little children in the playground. (He is still re-enacting aspects of his trauma.) In therapy, alongside kindness and warmth, the child is helped to process, feel, think and work through his inner-world conflict, pain and hurt to a point of resolution. His ghosts are then laid to rest, so that he no longer keeps unconsciously re-enacting his traumatic past, this time with other people as the victims. In a successful therapy the child will develop far richer ways of relating. He will develop other models of relationship based on kindness, empathy, co-operation and warmth.

One of the lovely things about child therapy or child counselling in infant and junior schools is that with younger 'toughies', behind their defences their hearts are often still open. So, with investment in therapy or counselling, it often does not take that long to reach the hurt or frightened child underneath. In one-to-one therapy, the vulnerable child who may have been a little horror in the classroom will often come out of hiding quite quickly. Because therapy provides such a concentrated time of empathy, children soon start showing a new tenderness and kindness in their play. In contrast, someone with, say, fifteen years of hardened defences, can be extremely difficult to reach. The internalised model of submission-dominance relating may have become too entrenched. It can be very difficult, and sometimes impossible, to entice the vulnerable, hurt or frightened child self out again. The older child may also stop the therapy, just when he is feeling that he is in danger of melting; or therapy may be avoided as it can be construed as just yet another 'power over' relationship. As one defensive adolescent said on flatly refusing therapy, 'I'm not giving someone that control over me'; 'Me saying all that about me and her just sitting there. No way.'

Therapy can help the bully or the hardened child to feel his hurt underneath in ways that make the pain bearable, so it no longer needs to be defended against. Without the safety of the psychological holding of a good therapist or counsellor, and the consistency of sessions week after week, the pain under a hardened heart is often far too much and far too deep for the child to dare to venture there alone. The mind's defence mechanisms will make sure of that.

For some children, therapy is the only way to make this shift away from 'big and tough' to the ability to use less drastic methods of protecting themselves, such as the capacity to say 'No'; to state their needs clearly; to negotiate, discuss or give feedback, so that they can remain open to love, feel moved and be tender and vulnerable, as appropriate.

Many children in counselling or therapy feel an exquisite relief in letting themselves become unburdened of the grief, hurt, rage, hate or fear they have been carrying around all by themselves, for far too long. Only then are many of them able to enter the delicious world of having softer, warmer, kinder feelings. As one little boy whose heart melted in therapy said, 'Funny, but it's like all the fighting inside me has stopped.'

Counselling or therapy is an excellent practice-ground for softer, less defensive ways of being. Hence the common situation of the therapist saying, 'But he's delightful' and the teacher saying, 'But he's a total nightmare', before the child has dared to take what he is experiencing or practising in the therapy room into the wider world.

What happens when children with hardened hearts start to melt

Stella, an eight-year-old bully who in counselling began to melt
For weeks, Stella enacted stories about an angry tiger who would devour, maim and kill. Then one day, the tiger surprisingly opened up a shop for children who didn't have very much. The tiger gave them lovely beds to sleep on and lovely friends to play with. When the counsellor asked, 'So how come tiger is different this week?', Stella said, *'Because something happened to the tiger's heart.'* Yes indeed. As a result of her counsellor's and teacher's tender concern for Stella, the tiger had developed a capacity for concern.

Sometimes a great deal of previously frozen unmet infantile need is released. Then, as in *A Nifflenoo Called Nevermind* (Sunderland & Armstrong, 2000), there may be some metaphorical floods and fires of feeling, especially when the child has been defending against intense grief:

> Turning one's self into stone . . . is a fairly common defence mechanism, as is turning into ice. I have treated two patients who described feeling like a block of ice. The difficulty with this defensive posture is that one can readily be melted with the heat of emotions and become nothing but a puddle of water. (Singer, 1977, p474)

If this happens, the child needs lots of warmth and empathy. He needs to feel both physically and psychologically held.

There can be that glorious moment in child therapy or counselling when the little toughie stops playing with soldiers and starts to get interested in such things as baby dolls and bottles. Usually, there is some sign of melting that occurs in the play. You get a little sign in a picture or in a sandplay of something far less defended: for example, the low-key presence of something small or soft, like a little cuddly ball in among a world of bombs and fighting. It shows you that the vulnerable little child underneath is still alive and ready to have a presence and a voice. But when he shows himself in this tentative way, do not press him to talk, or he might go away again. For an example of this new, far less defended self, look at the drawing of a sandplay in Figure 6. This sandplay was created by a child who had been bullying for years. After weeks of playing out one war after another, he did another picture of a war, but in the middle was a baby in a shopping trolley!

Often the bully or hardened-hearted child wants the counsellor or therapist at the beginning of the therapy to enact stories with a submission-dominance theme. Things like 'You be a stinky little mouse and I'll step on you' are not uncommon. But when a child is melting, the interactions change to co-operative 'power with' interactions. There is a new sense of ease in the therapeutic relationship, with lots of 'let's' and 'you and me together'. One therapist wrote in her notes about an eight-year-old ex-bully: 'We spend a lot of time now in gentle exchanges of whispering and humming.'

Figure 6
Drawing of a sandplay story told by a child who had bullied lots of children

People are alright as they are. There is nothing extra which they need in order to be whole – all that is necessary is for them to take down the shutters and the blinkers, and let the sun shine in. (Rowan, 1986, p11)

BIBLIOGRAPHY

Ainsworth MDS, Blehar MC, Waters E & Wall S, 1978, *Patterns of Attachment: A Psychological Study of the Strange Situation*, Lawrence Erlbaum Associates, Hillsdale, NJ.

Armstrong-Perlman E, 1995, Personal communication.

Auster P, 1988, *The Invention of Solitude*, Faber & Faber, London.

Bachelard G, 1969, *The Poetics of Space: The Classic Look at How We Experience Intimate Places*, Beacon Press, Boston. (Originally published in French, 1958)

Berne E, 1964, *Games People Play*, Grove Press, New York.

Blume ES, 1990, *Secret Survivors: Uncovering Incest and its After Effects in Women*, John Wiley, Chichester/New York.

Bowlby J, 1973, *Attachment and Loss: Volume 2 – Separation, Anxiety and Anger,* Hogarth Press, London.

Bowlby J, 1978, *Attachment and Loss: Volume 3 – Loss, Sadness and Depression*, Penguin, Harmondsworth.

Bowlby J, 1988, *A Secure Base: Clinical Applications of Attachment Theory*, Routledge, London.

Casement P, 1990, *Further Learning From the Patient: The Analytic Space and Process*, Tavistock/Routledge, London.

Chopra D, 1990, *Quantum Healing*, Bantam, New York.

Fairbairn WRD, 1940, 'Schizoid Factors in the Personality', pp3-27 in *Psychoanalytic Studies of the Personality* (1952), Tavistock/Routledge, London.

Frankl V, 1985, *Man's Search for Meaning*, Washington Square Press, New York. (Originally published in 1946)

Fromm E, 1973, *Anatomy of Human Destructiveness*, Cape, London.

Gallagher T, 1996, Talking about her writer husband Raymond Carver on BBC Radio 4, August.

Goodall J, 1988, *In the Shadow of Man*, 2nd edn, Weidenfeld & Nicolson, London.

Guntrip H, 1952, 'The Schizoid Personality and the External World', in *Harry Guntrip: Schizoid Phenomena, Object Relations and the Self*, 1992, H Karnac (Books) Ltd, London.

Harlow HF & Mears C, 1979, *Primate Perspectives*, John Wiley, New York/London.

Herman N, 1988, *My Kleinian Home: A Journey Through Four Psychotherapies*, Free Association Books, London.

Home Office, 1994, Chapter 4 in *Criminal Statistics England and Wales 1994*, HMSO, London.

Jeffers S, 1987, *Feel the Fear and Do it Anyway*, Arrow, London.

Jenner S, 1999, *The Parent/Child Game*, Bloomsbury, London.

Kafka F, 1981, *Stories 1904–1924* (Underwood JA, trans), Futura, London.

Keenan B, 1992, *An Evil Cradling*, Vintage, London.

Kohut H, 1977, *The Restoration of the Self*, International Universities Press, New York.

Levi P, 1984, 'Give Us' in *Primo Levi Collected Poems*, 1988, Faber & Faber, London.

Maslow AH, 1971, *The Farther Reaches of Human Nature*, Viking Penguin, New York.

Miller A, 1987, *For Your Own Good: The Roots of Violence in Child-Rearing*, (Hannum H & H, trans), Virago, London.

Milner M, 1987, *The Suppressed Madness of Sane Men*, Tavistock, London.

Mitchell S, 1988, *Relational Concepts in Psychoanalysis: An Integration*, Fifth Printing, New York.

Mollon P, 1993, *The Fragile Self: The Structure of Narcissistic Disturbance*, Whurr, London.

Pert CB, 1997, *Molecules of Emotion*, Simon & Schuster, London.

Polster E, 1987, *Every Person's Life is Worth a Novel*, New York, WW Norton, New York.

Polster E & Polster M, 1973, *Gestalt Therapy Integrated*, Brunner/Mazel, New York.

Randolph E, 1994, *Children Who Shock and Surprise: A Guide to Attachment Disorders*, RFR Publications, Cotati, Ca.

Robertson J & Robertson J, 1969, 'John – 17 Months: Nine Days in a Residential Nursery', 16mm film/video, The Robertson Centre; accompanied by a printed 'Guide to the Film' Series; British Medical Association/Concord Film Council.

Rowan J, 1986, *Ordinary Ecstasy: Humanistic Psychology in Action*, Routledge & Kegan Paul, London.

Schoenewolf G, 1991, *The Art of Hating*, Jason Aronson, Northvale, NJ.

Siegel DJ, 1999, *The Developing Mind*, The Guildford Press, New York.

Singer M, 1977, 'The Experience of Emptiness in Narcissistic and Borderline States: II. The Struggle for a Sense of Self and the Potential for Suicide', *International Review of Psycho-Analysis 4*: 471–477.

Stern DN, 1993, 'Acting versus Remembering in Transference Love and Infantile Love', in Spector Person E, Hagelin A & Fonagy P, eds, *On Freud's 'Observations on Transference-Love'*, Yale University Press, New Haven/London.

Stoppard T, 1967, *Rosencrantz and Guildenstern are Dead*, Faber & Faber, London.

Sunderland M, 1993, *Draw On Your Emotions*, Speechmark Publishing, Bicester.

Sunderland M, 2000, *Using Story Telling as a Therapeutic Tool with Children*, Speechmark Publishing, Bicester.

Sunderland M & Armstrong N, 2000, *A Nifflenoo Called Nevermind*, Speechmark Publishing, Bicester.

Thrail E, 1994, *Retrospect: The Story of an Analysis*, Quartet, London.

Troy M & Sroufe LA, 1987, 'Victimisation Among Preschoolers: Role of Attachment Relationship History', *Journal of American Academy of Child and Adolescent Psychiatry 26*: 166–172.

Van Der Kolk BA, 1989, 'The Compulsion to Repeat the Trauma: Re-enactment, Revictimisation and Masochism', *Psychiatric Clinics of North America*, 12: 389–411.

Weininger O, 1989, *Children's Phantasies: The Shaping of Relationships*, H Karnac (Books) Ltd, London.

Weininger O, 1993, *View from the Cradle: Children's Emotions in Everyday Life*, H Karnac (Books) Ltd, London.

Williams G, 1997, *Internal Landscapes and Foreign Bodies*, Tavistock, London.

Williamson M, 1992, *A Return to Love*, Random House, New York.

Winnicott DW, 1971, *Playing and Reality*, Penguin, Harmondsworth, New York.

De Zulueta F, 1993, *From Pain to Violence: The Traumatic Roots of Destructiveness*, Whurr, London.

Helping Children
With Feelings

Helping Children who have Hardened their Hearts or Become Bullies

A Guidebook